Content

MW00902919

How to Use This Book

Measurement is an engaging, hands-on resource to help students build the skills they need to become successful learners. By assessing and applying units of measurement, learners prepare themselves to tackle everyday tasks such as measuring out contents for a recipe or exchanging proper amounts of change when handling currency. Understanding how to measure and estimate measurements, such as weight, distance, volume, and quantities involving money, parallels educational trends that emphasize the development of learners' mathematical abilities. Through the understanding of different systems of measurement learners will develop their abilities in solving mathematical problems involving values, quantities, and distances.

Measurement is comprised of six sections, each emphasizing a different area of the third-grade math curriculum. Each section provides four curriculum-based activities, derived from standards of the National Council of Teachers of Mathematics (NCTM). The activities emphasize key math concepts and skills taught in classrooms across the United States. Each activity offers learners easy-to-comprehend directions as well as skill definitions and, when applicable, examples. The activities also present learner-friendly fun facts to help contextualize the mathematical concepts presented. Each of the following sections will help learners to develop their abilities in judging and converting measurements.

▭▷ Time and Temperature

In the third grade, learners build on their abilities to tell time and begin to evaluate time management. This is also the time learners begin to explore the measuring of temperature. Learners use tools, such as clocks, schedules, and thermometers, in order to enhance the mathematical skills that are an imperative part of being able to function in the real world.

▭▷ Area, Perimeter, Length, and Width

The second section of this book prompts learners to evaluate the space of items while exploring the relationships among the

© Rosen School Supply•Brain Builders Measurement•3•RSS

various measurements. The activities are geared to strengthen learners' understanding of space in terms of perimeter, area, length, and width. Being able to measure the space of items will be an invaluable tool for learners who later face problems involving geometry.

▨▷ Volume and Weight

In this section learners use the English and metric systems to evaluate and implement measurements of weight and volume. By understanding the various units of measurement, as well as the relationships these units have to one another, learners are prepared to use the tools necessary to solve mathematical problems involving quantity.

▨▷ Conversions

The fourth section focuses on the differences between the various units of distance, weight, and volume. Here, the activities concentrate on the relationships between units. By comparing units and drawing parallels between these mathematical concepts and everyday items, learners begin to relate better to systems of measurement.

▨▷ Money

In this section learners are challenged by problems that involve varying denominations of money. The activities in this section afford learners the opportunity to build a better understanding of how money works. By changing bills, looking at the different ways coins can be combined, and exploring the mathematical concept of profit, learners get a sound introduction to the practical applications of money.

▨▷ Estimating Measurements

The last section induces learners to draw on their knowledge of measurement to make judgments and then to use the proper tools to verify their suppositions. As learners make assessments and qualify their reasoning with proof, they reinforce their understanding of mathematical processes and how these processes are applied to measurement.

3

Name _____

Feel My Temperature Rising!

> **Directions: Look at the thermometer below and answer the following questions. Temperatures are in degrees Fahrenheit (°F).**

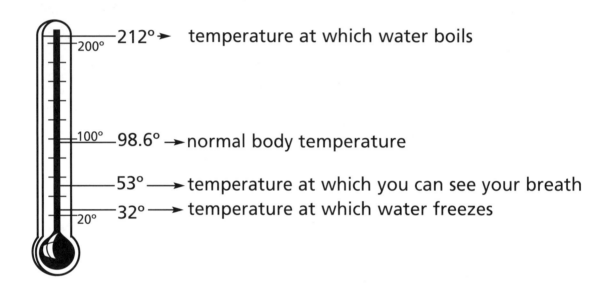

212° ➤ temperature at which water boils

98.6° ➤ normal body temperature

53° ➤ temperature at which you can see your breath

32° ➤ temperature at which water freezes

1 If the temperature is 12° F, how many degrees must it rise for water to boil?

_____

2A If the temperature outside is 60° F, how many degrees must it drop before you could go ice-skating?

    a 30

    b 22

    c 28

2B Explain why you chose this answer.

_____

4

Name _____

Sizing Things Up!

Example: Width (W) = 10

Length (L) = 12   Perimeter= (2 x 12) + (2 x 10) = 44

Directions: Find the perimeters for each rectangular shape. The formula to find the perimeter of a rectangle is Perimeter = (2 x L) + (2 x W).

Width = 6

Length = 4

1

Perimeter = _____

Width = 9

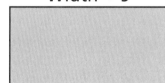

Length = 5

2

Perimeter = _____

Width = 12

Length = 2

3

Perimeter = _____

© Rosen School Supply•Brain Builders Measurement•3•RSS

Name _____

A Drop in the Bucket

> ✏️ **Directions: Look at the chart and circle the correct answers for the questions below.**

```
8 ounces = 1 cup
2 cups = 1 pint
2 pints = 1 quart
4 quarts = 1 gallon
```

1 If juice costs 75¢ for the quart-sized container and $2.79 for a gallon, which is the better buy?

   a the quart   **b** the gallon   **c** they are same

2 If you have 4 friends, what size container would be the right amount to give everyone one cup of juice?

   a cup   **b** pint   **c** quart

3 You invited 5 people over for lunch. If 2 of them want a cup of juice with their lunch, what size juice will you need?

   a cup   **b** pint   **c** quart

4 Jen and her brother Cliff each have two cups of water at breakfast, and another two cups each before they go to bed. How much water do the two of them drink in a day?

   a pint   **b** 2 quarts   **c** gallon

© Rosen School Supply•Brain Builders Measurement•3•RSS

Name _____

Weighing Your Options

The chart below shows 3 metric units and their approximate English equivalents.

> 1 kilogram (kg) is about 35 ounces.
>
> 30 grams (gm) is just a little more than an ounce.
>
> 3,000 milligrams (mg) is just a little more than an ounce.

Example: *You would measure the weight of a truck in kg.*

✏️➤ **Directions: From the chart above, choose the best unit of measurement for each item listed below. Choose kg, gm, or mg.**

1 You would measure the weight of a match in _____.

2 You would measure the weight of a book in_____.

3 You would measure the weight of a small piece of

thread in _____.

4 You would measure the weight of a train in_____.

5 You would measure the weight of a feather in_____.

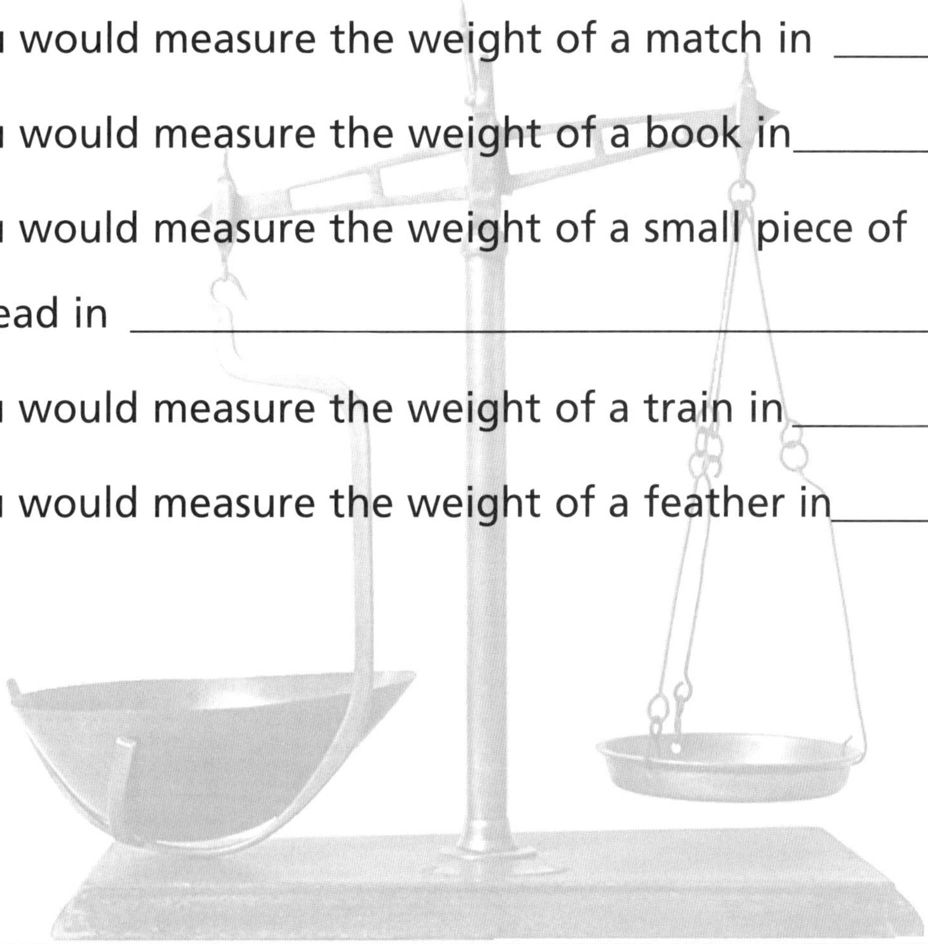

© Rosen School Supply•Brain Builders Measurement•3•RSS

Name _____

A Nickel for Your Thoughts

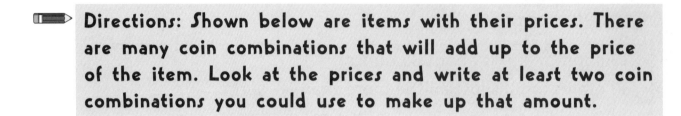

Directions: Shown below are items with their prices. There are many coin combinations that will add up to the price of the item. Look at the prices and write at least two coin combinations you could use to make up that amount.

Example: *$1.75*

quarters–3   *quarters–4*
dimes–5   *dimes–4*
nickels–10   *nickels–7*

1 $.75

quarters _____   quarters _____

dimes _____   dimes _____

nickels _____   nickels _____

2 $2.10

quarters _____   quarters _____

dimes _____   dimes _____

nickels _____   nickels _____

8

Name _____

Give Them an Inch

Directions: Look at the ruler below and estimate the length of each fish. Write in your estimate. Next, measure with a real ruler to see how close your estimate was. Write in the real length of the fish too.

Ruler markings: 1 2 3 4 5 6

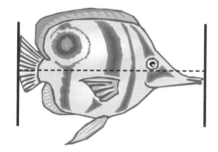

1 Estimate_____

   Measurement _____

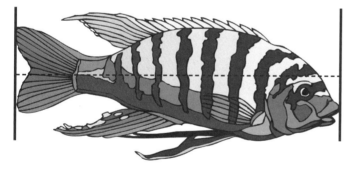

2 Estimate_____

   Measurement _____

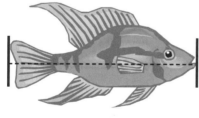

3 Estimate_____

   Measurement _____

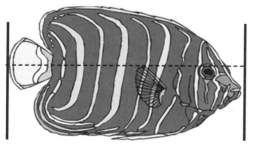

4 Estimate_____

   Measurement _____

9

Teaching Tips...

Background

• Telling time and temperature are perhaps the most commonly recurring mathematical concepts in our daily lives. Building these skills will help learners succeed at important everyday activities. Reinforcing these skills with exercises that challenge the learner to use what they know enhances cognitive skills of judgment and communication.

Homework Helper

• Using the time management activities on page 14 as a sample, have learners write down their daily schedule for a school day. It should include time for meals, school, sports, play, television, homework, and anything else that occurs.

Research-based Activity

• As an adjunct to Making Candy! (p. 13), have learners research the use of thermometers in cooking. They can do this in the library or on the Internet. The learner should make notes of at least five degree readings necessary for preparing certain dishes.

Test Prep

• The activities touch upon a broad base of national standards. The activities are geared toward preparing learners for life-broadening experiences and successful academic testing situations.

Different Audiences

• For challenged learners, use real clocks and thermometers as helpful tools for demonstration and reference. Such hands-on experience will add to their understanding of the activities in this section.

© Rosen School Supply•Brain Builders Measurement•3•RSS

Name _____

The Timely Prince

✏️ **Directions: Answer the following questions.**

1 An uncle gives his favorite niece a pet frog and a wristwatch for her birthday. Her wristwatch reads 11:30 A.M. Draw the hands on the clock that show this time.

2 The niece loves the frog. She kisses the frog on its forehead 3 hours and 30 minutes after 11:30. What time does her watch read now?

3 Draw the hands on the clock that show this new time.

4 The niece's frog magically turns into a prince five hours later. What time does her watch now read?

5 Draw the hands on the clock that show this time.

© Rosen School Supply•Brain Builders Measurement•3•RSS

Name _____

How Hot Is It?

> ✏️ **Directions: Look at the thermometer below and answer the following questions. Temperatures are in degrees Fahrenheit (°F).**

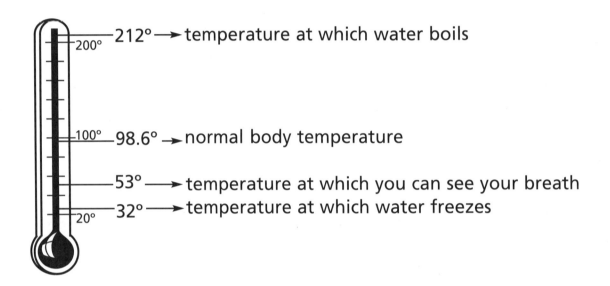

212° → temperature at which water boils

98.6° → normal body temperature

53° → temperature at which you can see your breath

32° → temperature at which water freezes

1 Your thermometer reads 32° F. Then the temperature drops 12 degrees and then climbs back up 40 degrees. What temperature is it now?

_____

2 If the outside temperature is 42° F, how many degrees must the temperature drop in order for water to freeze?

_____

FUN FACT The toothfish lives in the Antarctic Ocean. It grows to 6 feet. It produces its own antifreeze so it can live in near-freezing water.

12

Name _____

Making Candy!

To the right is a thermometer that shows the temperatures needed to make three different candies. Temperatures are in degrees Fahrenheit (°F).

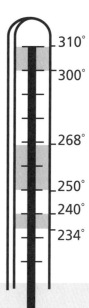

Candy	Temperature
soft ball	234° to 240°
hard ball	250° to 268°
brittle threads	300° to 310°

Directions: Look at the thermometer and then answer the following questions.

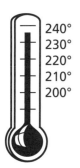

1 Tad is heating up a mix and has reached the temperature shown on the thermometer on the left. What kind of candy is he probably trying to make?

_____

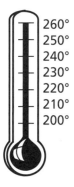

2 Tad has heated a candy mix to 260°. What kind of candy is he making?

_____

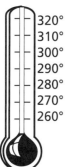

3 An order just came in for brittle thread candy. On the thermometer to the left, fill in the temperature that Tad needs to heat his mix to.

13

Name _____

Tina's Schedule

Below is Tina's Saturday schedule.

Task	Time
Eat breakfast	9:30 to 10:00 A.M.
Practice piano	10:00 A.M. to 12:00 P.M.
Lunch	12:00 to 1:00 P.M.
Play with friends	1:00 to 5:00 P.M.
Dinner	5:00 to 6:00 P.M.
Work on computer	6:00 to 8:30 P.M.
Shower and go to bed	8:30 to 9:00 P.M.

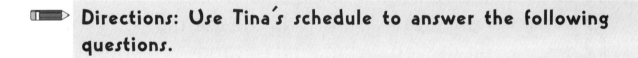

Directions: Use Tina's schedule to answer the following questions.

1 What time is Tina halfway through eating her breakfast?

_____

2 How many hours has Tina scheduled for playing with friends and practicing the piano?

_____

3 What is the total number of hours and minutes Tina has scheduled for eating breakfast, lunch, and dinner?

_____

© Rosen School Supply•Brain Builders Measurement•3•RSS

Name _____

Skill Check—Time and Temperature

Telling Time

 Directions: Answer the following questions.

1 2 hours before 12:00 P.M. is __:_ _A.M. Draw in the hands that show this time on the clock.

2 3 hours after 3:00 A.M. is __:_ _A.M. Draw in the hands that show this time on the clock.

Understanding Temperature

1 Your thermometer reads 62° F. The temperature drops 12 degrees and then climbs 30 degrees. Write the final temperature.

_____

2 If the outside temperature is 62° F, how many degrees must the temperature drop in order for water to freeze?

_____

15

© Rosen School Supply•Brain Builders Measurement•3•RSS

Teaching Tips...

Background

• Understanding mathematical concepts involving dimensions and space allows the learner to make connections between mathematical theory and everyday tasks that involve problem solving. Using basic shapes to explore perimeter and area will give the learner the opportunity to apply a formula to achieve a goal. At the same time, it will introduce the learner to problems that require a basic understanding of dimensional relationships. Applying these ideas to develop generalizations, solve problems, and practice the skills involved will prepare the learners for more advanced concepts of geometry.

Homework Helper

• As per Picture Frames (p. 18), have learners determine the measurements of three framed pictures they find at home. They should measure both the dimensions of the frame and the pictures.

Research-based Activity

• Using the questions from Redecorating (p. 19) as prompts, ask the learner to redesign the classroom or a room in his or her home. Using objects in the rooms, have the learner determine the areas of rugs, tables, and other furnishings.

Test Prep

• The activities incorporate strategies commonly found on standardized tests nationwide. Familiarity with such strategies helps prepare learners for test-taking situations.

Different Audiences

• Challenged learners may benefit from the hands-on experience of configuring area, perimeter, length, and width of everyday objects. Working with learners using objects such as envelopes, photos, doors, and mirrors will help learners apply their measuring skills.

© Rosen School Supply•Brain Builders Measurement•3•RSS

Name _____

Building Blocks

Length and width are used to find the perimeter of a rectangle. Length is represented by L. Width is represented by W. The formula to find the perimeter of a rectangle is Perimeter=(2 x L) + (2 x W).

Example: Width (W) = 8

Length (L) = 12   *Perimeter = (2 x 12) + (2 x 8) = 40*

 Directions: Find the perimeters for each rectangular shape.

Width = 16

1

Length = 8

Perimeter = _____

Width = 16

2

Length = 4

Perimeter = _____

Width = 12

3 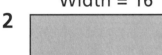 Length = 3

Perimeter = _____

© Rosen School Supply•Brain Builders Measurement•3•RSS

Name _____

Picture Frames

Lita wants to frame three different drawings. Before she can, however, she needs to know the size of each drawing.

Directions: Write the correct measurements for the three different drawings in the spaces below.

Picture 1	Picture 2	Picture 3
Length _____	Length _____	Length _____
Width _____	Width _____	Width _____

© Rosen School Supply•Brain Builders Measurement•3•RSS

Name _____

Area

Redecorating

Tina has decided to wallpaper her bedroom. First she must find the area she needs to cover. The formula to find area is Area = Length x Width.

✏️➡️ **Directions: Use the picture below to find the following areas.**

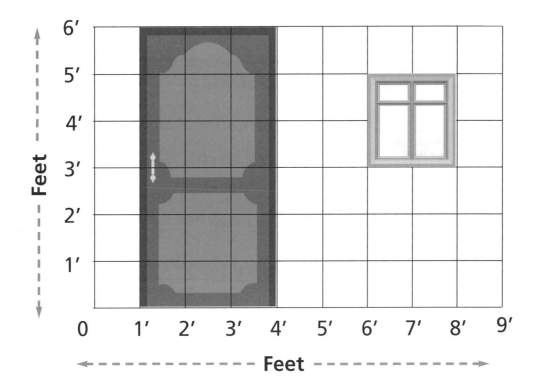

1 What is the area of the door? _____

2 What is the area of the window? _____

Interior designers use small pictures of furniture to help them design. This way, they can design a room without having to move the actual chairs, couches, and dressers around.

© Rosen School Supply•Brain Builders Measurement•3•RSS

High Traffic Area

Finding the areas of everyday objects such as road signs can be fun. To find the area of a rectangle or a square, multiply its length by its width (or side by side).

Example: Area of rectangle = Length (L) x Width (W)

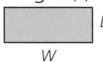

Area of square = Side (S) x Side (S)

> **Directions: Find the length, width, and area of each road sign below. Your answers should be in inches.**

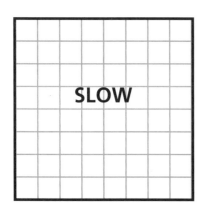

SLOW
1A Length _____

B Width _____

C Area _____

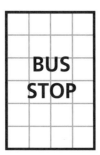

BUS STOP
2A length _____

B Width _____

C Area _____

Areas of land found by length times width are rough measures. That's because Earth's surface is curved.

© Rosen School Supply•Brain Builders Measurement•3•RSS

Name _____

Skill Check—Area, Perimeter, Length, and Width

Perimeter

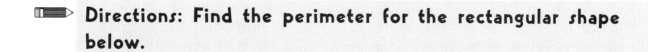

Directions: Find the perimeter for the rectangular shape below.

Width = 6

Length = 10

Perimeter = _____

Length and Width

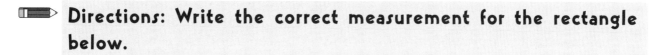

Directions: Write the correct measurement for the rectangle below.

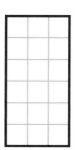

Length = _____

Width = _____

Area

Directions: Find the area for the rectangular shape below.

Width = 5"

Length = 10"

Area = _____

© Rosen School Supply•Brain Builders Measurement•3•RSS

Teaching Tips...

Background

• Understanding the different units of measurement for volume and weight provides learners with the tools they need to solve everyday problems. Building these skills will help learners succeed at common tasks. Practical exercises, which challenge the learners to use what they know, enhance skills of judgment and reinforce the learner's understanding of relationships between units of measurement.

Homework Helper

• To add to the volume exercises on pages 23, 24, and 25, have learners ask an adult at home to include them the next time cup measurements are taken in preparing a meal. Also, ask learners to list five items and their volumes at home that have their volumes printed on the labels.

Research-based Activity

• Ask learners to accompany their parents to the grocery store. Have them find as many items as they can that are packaged in different units of measurement. Have them write down the items and the units of measurement.

Test Prep

• The activities included are intended to give the learner practice evaluating information and applying it to solve problems. The activities draw upon many state standards and are designed to develop test-taking skills and problem-solving abilities.

Different Audiences

• For the challenged learner, have him or her transfer contents from a smaller measuring implement, such as a cup, into the next larger implement, such as a pint, and so on. Have them count out loud the units as they are being transferred.

TEACHING TIPS

© Rosen School Supply•Brain Builders Measurement•3•RSS

Name _____

So Many Cups!

Volume is the measurement of how much something can hold. We use ounces, cups, pints, quarts, and gallons to measure liquids.

> 8 ounces = 1 cup
> 2 cups = 1 pint
> 2 pints = 1 quart
> 4 quarts = 1 gallon

Directions: Use the chart above to answer the following questions.

Example: *Judy spilled 3 cups of milk. How many ounces is this?*
  Answer: 24

1 Joe drinks $1\frac{1}{2}$ gallons of juice. How many quarts is that?

_____

2 The kitchen faucet leaks 8 ounces of water per hour. How many cups of water does it leak per day?

_____

3 Aunt Judy puts soup in jars in order to store them. If she has 5 jars that each hold 1 quart, how many pints of soup can she store? How many cups?

_____ pints   _____ cups

© Rosen School Supply•Brain Builders Measurement•3•RSS

Name _____

Daily Milk

In everyday life, it is important to be able to estimate volume.

 Directions: Circle the correct answers.

Example: *The container of milk in Jose's refrigerator has 2 cups of milk in it. About how much milk is that?*

   a) pint   b) quart   c) gallon

1 If milk costs $1.00 for the quart-sized container and $3.39 for the gallon, which is the better buy?

   a quart   **b** gallon   **c** the same

2 It's cookie time for you and your friends. If you have 11 friends, what size carton would you need to give everyone a cup of milk?

   a pint   **b** quart   **c** gallon

3 You invited 7 people to your tea party. If 5 of them want a little milk in their tea, what size milk will you need?

   a pint   **b** quart   **c** gallon

4 Jenny and her brother Tony each have a cup of milk at breakfast and another cup before they go to bed. How much milk do the two of them drink in a day?

   a pint   **b** quart   **c** gallon

© Rosen School Supply•Brain Builders Measurement•3•RSS

Name _____

She's Got the Juice

✏️ **Directions:** Matilda is serving juice to her friends. Look at the chart below and then answer the following questions.

> 16 ounces = 1 pint
> 32 ounces = 1 quart
> 128 ounces = 1 gallon

Example: *If Matilda's friend Steve drinks 16 ounces of orange juice, how many pints is that?* <u>Answer:</u> 1 pint

1 Matilda has a quart of apple juice. Joan and Leon drink 16 ounces of it. How many ounces does Matilda have left?

_____

2 Matilda's friends want to combine 32 ounces of grape juice with 16 ounces of cranberry juice. How many pints of juice would this be?

_____

3 If Matilda starts with a gallon of mango juice and her friends drink 1 quart of it, how many ounces of juice would she have left?

_____

A gallon of water weighs about 8 pounds. A gallon of gasoline weighs about 6 pounds.

© Rosen School Supply•Brain Builders Measurement•3•RSS

Name _____

Which Weighs More?

Directions: Draw a line from the weight to the drawing on the left that matches it.

2 pounds

10 pounds

2,500 pounds

700 pounds

20 pounds

FUN FACT

Did you know that there is a unit of measurement called the dram? There are 16 drams in an ounce.

© Rosen School Supply•Brain Builders Measurement•3•RSS

Name _____

Skill Check—Volume and Weight

Understanding Volume

✏️ **Directions: Use the chart below to answer the following questions.**

8 ounces = 1 cup
2 cups = 1 pint
2 pints = 1 quart
4 quarts = 1 gallon

Tom's birdbath can hold 2 gallons of liquid. He pours in 4 quarts of water. How many more quarts of water will he need to fill it?

_____

Estimating Weight

✏️ **Directions: Draw a line from the weight to the drawing on the left that matches it.**

600 pounds

140 pounds

4 pounds

27

Teaching Tips...

Background

• It is essential for learners to build a strong foundation of skills for converting units of measurement. The ability to recognize the connections between units and to be able to quickly and concisely assess quantity is a vital skill for learners at this level. Providing unit examples with which learners can identify will make conversions more accessible to them.

Homework Helper

• Have students read the labels of five items in their kitchen cupboards. Have them list measurements using the English system and its metric equivalents.

Research-based Activity

• Have the learners measure certain objects in the room with a metric ruler and then report their findings.

Test Prep

• The strategies incorporated in these activities are designed to help students draw upon guidelines recommended by many state standards. The activities aim to help learners select wisely and solve problems, becoming better test takers and better at math applications.

Different Audiences

• Focus more on the exercises that involve English units of measurement with English-as-a-Second-Language learners because they are more likely to be familiar with the metric system.

TEACHING TIPS

28

Name _____

Judging Distance

We can measure distance in inches, feet, or miles. We can also measure distance using metric units such as kilometers, meters, centimeters, and millimeters. This chart shows metric units and their approximate equivalents.

kilometer (km)	about half a mile
meter (m)	about 3 feet
centimeter (cm)	about the width of your forefinger
millimeter (mm) (1,000 of these make a meter.)	about the width of thin lead in a mechanical pencil

Directions: Fill in the blanks with your best choice.

1 The distance from your neighbor's nose to his fingertips is

about 1 _____.

2 The distance from your garage door to a store ten blocks

away is about 1 _____.

3 The length of a pencil could be about 20 _____.

4 The width of a pencil could be about 1 _____.

5 A centipede has many legs. It's creepy, too. Its length is

about 35 _____.

© Rosen School Supply•Brain Builders Measurement•3•RSS

Name _____

Liter or Millileter?

Volume is the amount of space that something takes up. Metric units can be used to measure volume. This chart shows two metric units and their equivalents in ounces.

liter (l)	33.8 ounces
100 milliliters (ml)	3.38 ounces

Directions: Below is a series of statements. Answer whether they are true or false.

Example: *If you wanted to measure the amount of water in a water tower you would want to use milliliters.* <u>Answer</u>: *false*

1 If you wanted to measure the liquid in a teaspoon, you would use milliliters._____

2 If you wanted to measure the liquid in a barrel, you would use liters._____

3 If you wanted to measure the amount of jet fuel in an airplane, you would want to use milliliters._____

4 If you wanted to measure the amount of water in a swimming pool, you would use liters._____

© Rosen School Supply•Brain Builders Measurement•3•RSS

Name _____

Weigh Station

We can measure weight using ounces, pounds, or tons. We can also use metric units to measure weight.
This chart shows three metric units and their approximate equivalents.

kilogram (kg)	about 35 ounces
30 grams (gm)	about a little more than an ounce
3000 milligrams (mg)	about a little more than an ounce

✏️ **Directions: Choose the best unit of measurement (kg, gm, mg) for each item listed below.**

Example: *A car would be measured in kilograms.*

1 You would measure the weight of an airplane in _____.

2 You would measure the weight of a small piece of yarn

   in _____.

3 You would measure the weight of a volleyball in _____.

4 You would measure the weight of a bicycle in _____.

FUN FACT

Milligrams are saved for tiny measures. A scale used to measure milligrams can give bad readings if even a fingerprint or two is left on the scale.

31

Name _____

The Longest Mile

Being able to judge distance becomes easier when you better understand the units we use to measure.
The most standard units of distance are as follows:

mile	1,720 yards or 5,280 feet
yard	3 feet
foot	12 inches
inch	about the length of a child's nose

Directions: Write the unit of distance you might best use to measure the following.

Example: *The distance between New York City and Denver is measured in miles.*

1 The fence around a backyard _____

2 The height of a traffic sign _____

3 The length of a toy car _____

4 The width of a television _____

5 The distance of the International Space Station above

the earth _____

6 Estimating the distance an inchworm might crawl in

a minute _____

A golfer will often measure how many yards away an object is. He'll measure by pacing. Each step equals about a yard.

© Rosen School Supply•Brain Builders Measurement•3•RSS

Name _____

Skill Check—Conversions

Metric Distance

This chart shows metric units and their approximate equivalents.

kilometer (km)	about half a mile
meter (m)	about 3 feet
centimeter (cm)	about the width of your forefinger
millimeter (mm)	about the width of thin lead in a mechanical pencil

Directions: Fill in the blank with your best choice.

1 The width of a piece of licorice would be about 8 _____wide.

2 The width of a car might be 2 _____wide.

Understanding Distances

mile	1,720 yards, or 5,280 feet
yard	3 feet
foot	12 inches
inch	about the length of a child's nose

Directions: Write the unit of distance you might use to measure the following.

1 The length of a stuffed animal _____

2 The distance between towns _____

© Rosen School Supply•Brain Builders Measurement•3•RSS

Teaching Tips...

Background

• Learners who understand denominations of currency and the values they represent will be prepared for everyday practical tasks involving money. Furthermore, learners will strengthen their understanding of quantities and values that will later be directly applied to more sophisticated mathematical concepts such as fractions, percentages, and statistics. By challenging the learner with exercises that involve money values, the learner sharpens his or her tools of quantitative reasoning.

Homework Helper

• Have learners make colored drawings of a piece of currency, such as a dollar bill. Then ask the learners to describe or show all the ways of making the equivalent of a dollar bill—4 quarters, 10 dimes, etc.

Research-based Activity

• To build on the Understanding Profit activity (p. 37), set up a scenario in which the learner is the proprietor of a business, buying and selling items found in the house or school.

Test Prep

• The following activities are geared to prepare learners for everyday experiences and successful academic testing situations.

Different Audiences

• For the accelerated learner, a calculator may encourage exploration into areas that might otherwise be avoided because they involve repetitive work.

© Rosen School Supply•Brain Builders Measurement•3•RSS

Name _____

Spare Change

✏️ **Directions:** Shown below are items with their prices. There are many coin combinations that will add up to the price of the item. Look at the prices of the items and write in at least two coin combinations you could use to make up that amount.

Example: *$1.50*

quarters–3   quarters–4
dimes–5   dimes–4
nickels–5   nickels–2

1 1.75

quarters_____   quarters_____

dimes _____   dimes _____

nickels _____   nickels _____

2 $2.50

quarters_____   quarters_____

dimes _____   dimes _____

nickels _____   nickels _____

FUN FACT Normally, a dime is worth two nickels. However, the quite rare 1916 D dime might even get you a new car. The coin is worth $35,000!

© Rosen School Supply•Brain Builders Measurement•3•RSS

Name _____

Lost and Found

> ✏️ **Directions:** Your mom tells you that you can keep half of the coins you find under the couch. Write in how much you earn if you find...

	You Find	You Keep
1	_____	_____
2	_____	_____
3	_____	_____
4	_____	_____

FUN FACT If your parent says you are a nuisance, then you must act better. But if you are called a numismatic, that's something else—an expert on coins.

© Rosen School Supply•Brain Builders Measurement•3•RSS

Name _____

We're in the Money!

A profit is what you earn after paying off your expenses.

Example: *You sell baseball cards. They cost you 25¢ each. That's your expense. If you sell them for 35¢ each then your profit is 10¢ per card.*

 **Directions: Below are some items you are selling at your sidewalk sale. Find the profits for each item.**

1 Chocolate Cookies

Expense per cookie = 10¢

Selling price per cookie = 20¢

Profit per cookie = _____

Profit per 100 cookies = _____

2 Old Toys

Expense per item = 0¢

Selling price per item = 30¢

Profit for each toy = _____

Profit for 20 toys = _____

3 Baseball Cards

Expense per card = 75¢

Selling price per card = $1.00

Profit per card = _____

Profit per 100 cards = _____

FUN FACT Tom Golisano began the Paychex company with $3,000. Now he's worth over $1,000,000,000. (That's a billion dollars!)

© Rosen School Supply•Brain Builders Measurement•3•RSS

Name _____

Breaking a Twenty

Store clerks try to give change to their customers in the largest units possible.

Example: If a customer's change is $5.25, the clerk will try to give the customer a $5 bill and a quarter.

> ✏️ **Directions: Look at the amount given to the clerk. Then help the clerk figure out the largest units of change to give back to the customer.**

Price of item	Bill given to clerk	Change returned
1 $14.00	$20 dollar bill	_____
2 $18.95	$20 dollar bill	_____
3 $8.95	$10 dollar bill	_____
4 $.95	$5 dollar bill	_____
5 $14.25	$20 dollar bill	_____

© Rosen School Supply•Brain Builders Measurement•3•RSS

Name _____

Skill Check—Money

Coin Combinations

✏️➡ **Directions: Look at the prices and write a coin combination you could use to make up that amount.**

1 $2.75

quarters_____

dimes_____

nickels_____

2 $1.15

quarters_____

dimes_____

nickels_____

Understanding Profit

✏️➡ **Directions: Below are some items you are selling. Find the profits for each item.**

1 Lemonade

Expense per drink = 10¢
Selling price per drink = 25¢
Profit per drink = 15¢

Profit for 10 drinks = _____

2 Iced Tea

Expense per drink = 5¢
Selling price per drink = 25¢
Profit per drink = 20¢

Profit for 10 drinks = _____

© Rosen School Supply•Brain Builders Measurement•3•RSS

Teaching Tips...

TEACHING TIPS

Background
• A learner's skills of reason and judgment are reinforced when exercises that use estimation and proof are mastered. Learner's abilities to make accurate assessments help them with the processes used for problem solving. Implementing systems of measure to justify their conjectures will strengthen learners' understanding of measurements.

Homework Helper
• Have the learners estimate distances that are familiar to them, such as the walk from their front steps/yard to their front door. Then have them measure these distances to check their estimations. Have a general discussion about their findings.

Research-based Activity
• Have the learners find a local map of a place close to school or home. This might be found in the library or on the Internet. Have the learners chart and measure distances between different points on the map.

Test Prep
• The use of estimation enhances confidence in approaching problems of all kinds. If the learner can envision the correct approach to solving a problem, then the student can focus on solving the problem with confidence. Test-taking skills are enhanced when the learner can quickly approximate—within a nominal margin of error—answers to math questions.

Different Audiences
• Challenged learners might play a game in a group setting in which they estimate distances that can be measured and confirmed in the classroom, such as "How high is the ceiling in feet?"

© Rosen School Supply•Brain Builders Measurement•3•RSS

Name _____

Inch by Inch

✏️ **Directions:** Look at the ruler below and estimate the length of each item. Write down your estimate. Then measure with a real ruler to see how close your guess was.

| 1 | 2 | 3 | 4 | 5 | 6 |

1

Estimate _____

Measurement _____

2

Estimate _____

Measurement _____

© Rosen School Supply•Brain Builders Measurement•3•RSS

Name _____

The Other Side of the Ruler

> Directions: The ruler below measures centimeters. Estimate the animals' lengths in centimeters. Write down your estimate. Then measure with a real ruler to see how close your guess was.

1 Estimate _____

Measurement _____

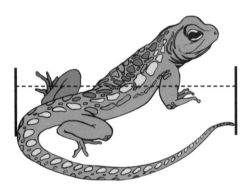

2 Estimate _____

Measurement _____

3 Estimate _____

Measurement _____

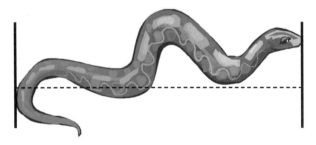

4 Estimate _____

Measurement _____

© Rosen School Supply•Brain Builders Measurement•3•RSS

Name _____

Guess the Weight

> **Directions: Look at the following questions and circle the best answer.**

1 The weight of a soccer ball is:
  a less than 5 pounds.
  b between 10 and 20 pounds.
  c greater than twenty pounds.

2 The weight of a full-grown polar bear is:
  a 25 to 100 pounds.
  b 775 to 1,500 pounds.
  c 3,000 to 4,500 pounds.

3 The weight of an adult chimpanzee is:
  a 10 to 25 pounds.
  b 120 to 150 pounds.
  c 775 to 1,500 pounds.

4 The weight of an elephant is:
  a 85 to 110 pounds.
  b 8,000 to 15,000 pounds.
  c 100,000 to 300,000 pounds.

5 The weight of a full-grown horse is:
  a 900 to 1,100 pounds.
  b 300 to 500 pounds.
  c 35 to 350 pounds.

The largest tiger in recorded history weighed 904 pounds!

© Rosen School Supply•Brain Builders Measurement•3•RSS

Name _____

So Little Time

It is often important to be able to estimate the time it will take to do something in order to manage your schedule.

 Directions: Look at the following list of activities and the times when each activity begins. Then draw a line from the time the activity begins to the time when it is finished.

Eating breakfast

Watching a movie

Raking leaves in the yard

Brushing your teeth

© Rosen School Supply•Brain Builders Measurement•3•RSS

Name _____

Skill Check—Estimating Measurements

Estimating Inches

✏️ **Directions:** Look at the ruler below. Estimate the length of each item. Write down your estimate. Then measure with a real ruler to see how close your guess was.

| 1 | 2 | 3 | 4 | 5 | 6 |

1 Estimate _____

Measurement _____

2 Estimate _____

Measurement _____

Estimating Centimeters

✏️ **Directions:** Look at the ruler below. Estimate the length of each item. Write down your estimate. Then measure with a real ruler to see how close your guess was.

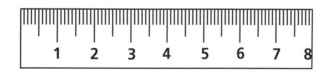

| 1 | 2 | 3 | 4 | 5 | 6 | 7 | 8 |

1 Estimate _____

Measurement _____

2 Estimate _____

Measurement _____

45

© Rosen School Supply•Brain Builders Measurement•3•RSS

Answer Key

p. 4
1) 200 degrees
2A) c
  B) Answers will vary.

p. 5
1) (2 x 4) + (2 x 6) = 20
2) (2 x 5) + (2 x 9) = 28
3) (2 x 2) + (2 x 12) = 28

p. 6
1) b
2) c
3) b
4) b

p. 7
1) gm
2) gm
3) mg
4) kg
5) mg

p. 8
1) quarters–2   quarters–1
   dimes–2   dimes–4
   nickels–1   nickels–2

Other answers will vary.

2) quarters–8   quarters–6
   dimes–0   dimes–5
   nickels–2   nickels–2

Other answers will vary.

p. 9
A) Estimations will vary.
Measurement = 2 inches

B) Estimations will vary.
Measurement = 3.5 inches

C) Estimations will vary.
Measurement = 2 inches

D) Estimations will vary.
Measurement = 2.5 inches

p. 11
1)

2) 3:00
3)

4) 8:00
5)

p. 12
1) 60° F
2) 10

p. 13
1) soft ball
2) hard ball
3)

320°
310°
300°
290°
280°
270°
260°

p. 14
1) 9:45
2) 6
3) 2 hours and 30 minutes

p. 15
Telling Time
1) 10:00

2) 6:00

**Understanding
Temperature**
1) 80° F
2) 30

p.17
1) (2 x 8) + (2 x 16) = 48
2) (2 x 4) + (2 x 16) = 40
3) (2 x 3) + (2 x 12) = 30

p.18
1) Length 10" Width 7"
2) Length 12" Width 9"
3) Length 8" Width 6"

p. 19
1) 18 square feet
2) 4 square feet

46

p. 20

1A) 8 inches

 B) 8 inches

 C) 64 square inches

2A) 6 inches

 B) 4 inches

 C) 24 square inches

p. 21

Perimeter

Perimeter=

(2 x 10) + (2 x 6) = 32

Length and Width

Length = 6   Width = 3

Area

Area = 50 square inches

p. 23

1) 6

2) 24

3) 10 pints, 20 cups

p. 24

1) b

2) c

3) a

4) b

p. 25

1) 16

2) 3

3) 96

p. 26

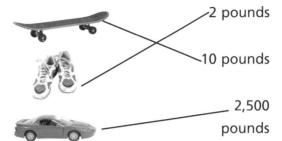

2 pounds

10 pounds

2,500 pounds

700 pounds

20 pounds

p. 27

Understanding Volume

4

Estimating Weight

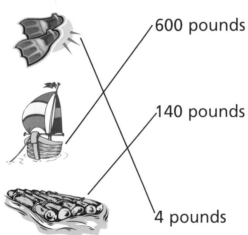

600 pounds

140 pounds

4 pounds

p. 29

1) meter

2) kilometer

3) centimeters

4) centimeter

5) millimeters

p. 30

1) true

2) true

3) false

4) true

p. 31

1) kilograms (kg)

2) milligrams (mg)

3) grams (gm)

4) kilograms (kg)

p. 32

1) yards

2) feet

3) inches

4) inches

5) miles

6) inches

p. 33

Metric Distances

1) millimeters (mm)

2) meters (m)

Understanding Distances

1) inches

2) miles

p. 35

1)

quarters–6	quarters–4
dimes–2	dimes–7
nickels–1	nickels–1

(Other answers will vary.)

© Rosen School Supply•Brain Builders Measurement•3•RSS

2) quarters–8   quarters–6
   dimes–4   dimes–8
   nickels–2   nickels–4

(Other answers will vary.)

p. 36
1) 80¢, 40¢
2) $1.10, 55¢
3) 80¢, 40¢
4) 90¢, 45¢

p. 37
1) 10¢, $10.00
2) 30¢, $6.00
3) 25¢, $25.00

p. 38
1) one $5 bill and one $1 bill
2) one $1 bill and one nickel
3) one $1 bill and one nickel
4) four $1 bills and one nickel
5) one $5 bill and three quarters

p. 39
Coin Combinations
1) quarters–8
   dimes–7
   nickels–1
(Other answers will vary.)

2) quarters–4
   dimes–1
   nickels–1
(Other answers will vary.)

Understanding Profit
1) $1.50
2) $2.00

p. 41
1) Estimates vary.
   Measurement = $2\frac{1}{2}$ inches
2) Estimates vary.
   Measurement = 2 inches

p. 42
1) Estimates vary.
   Measurement = 4 cm
2) Estimates vary.
   Measurement = 6 cm
3) Estimates vary.
   Measurement = 3 cm
4) Estimates vary.
   Measurement = 8 cm

p. 43
1) a
2) b
3) b
4) b
5) a

p. 44

p. 45
Estimating Inches
1) Estimates vary.
   Measurement = 2 inches
2) Estimates vary.
   Measurement = 3 inches

Estimating Centimeters
1) Estimates vary.
   Measurement = 7 cm
2) Estimates vary.
   Measurement = 6 cm

© Rosen School Supply•Brain Builders Measurement•3•RSS